trailriding tips
& techniques
from glentress

ESSENTIALS

The author and publisher have made every effort to ensure that the information in this publication is accurate, and accept no responsibility whatsoever for any loss, injury, inconvenience or punctures experienced by any person or persons whilst using this book.

published by
pocket mountains ltd
6 Church Wynd, Bo'ness EH51 0AN
pocketmountains.com

ISBN-13: 978-0-9554548-4-4

Printed in Poland

Introduction

The growth in mountain biking across Scotland in recent years has been nothing less than spectacular. Riders now come from far and wide not just to test themselves on the purpose-built single-track at mountain bike centres around the country, but also to experience an almost unlimited variety of natural trails - often in areas of outstanding beauty.

Our base at Glentress in the Scottish Borders demonstrates just how popular the sport has become. When it opened in 2002, the Hub welcomed around 90,000 visitors during its first full year. Today, that figure is closer to 330,000.

When we first opened the Hub, we were at the tail end of our professional racing careers and thought we would spend our days just riding our bikes and teaching other riders. However, having underestimated the hard work and long hours involved in running our own

business, it was not until a couple of years ago that we were able to emerge from beneath the mountains of paperwork and actually spend time with the people who were riding the trails.

The first thing that struck us was that although a lot of riders were quick, they lacked some of the essential foundation skills required. Over time, the idea to offer essential skills training days gradually took root - days that have since proved immensely popular not just for riders with years of experience behind them, but also those starting out on their first mountain bike adventures.

Similarly, this book is for both categories of rider. Following a similar format to our training days, it provides a back-to-basics approach that helps build a layer of skills

that will enable riders of all abilities to progress. Starting with advice on choosing and then setting up a mountain bike, the pages that follow outline fundamental techniques that will transform your riding and take you to a much higher level than you will have ever thought possible.

Crucially, developing a foundation layer of skills also helps remove much of the fear factor when riding - regardless of experience. As such, this book will give you the knowledge and technical ability to cope with almost anything that the trail throws at you.

Practice, practice, practice

The spirit of this book and everything we do at Glentress is about enjoying your riding and trying new things. Those familiar with the set-up will have noticed that the riders that appear to have the most skill and confidence are usually found hanging out at the Freeride Park. The very nature of the Freeride area encourages practice - often a short run over the same obstacles again and again - and many of these riders spend the whole day working on their fundamental skills. Once confident with the fundamentals, you, too, can begin to try new things and get creative. Watch how others ride a particular obstacle and then try it for yourself. There is always an opportunity to learn. We have been out with kids clubs and followed 10-year-olds down lines that we had never even considered.

By thinking about your riding from a different point of view, you will constantly challenge and surprise yourself. You will also be amazed at the difference it makes to your riding ability - and enjoyment.

Fit to ride

Technique is one thing, but you also need a reasonable level of fitness to get the most out of trailriding. Mountain biking, after all, can be quite stressful on your body. It is a workout of extremes with your heart rate increasing rapidly on the uphill sections and then flattening on the downhill. As such, it is important to build a base level of fitness. After all, if you have nothing left at the top of every hill, it will affect your performance on the tricky downhill sections.

Fortunately, you don't have to put in loads of miles to build a solid base. A 30-minute ride to work two or three times per week would be a good start. It is also better to build a base by doing some easier riding where your body is not constantly being stressed. Road riding is perfect as you can maintain an even tempo and a constant heart rate. And don't worry about needing a road bike. Just buy some slick tyres for your mountain bike. That way you get to train the same muscles in the same position as you would use when trailriding.

It is also advisable to have a good pre-ride warm-up. For most of us, this means building up the intensity at the start of the ride, so go easy to begin with. If you ride with people who like to hammer it from the outset, try to arrive 15 minutes or so earlier and do your own preparation.

Fuelling up

For any kind of sustained exercise it is important to eat a balanced diet and be properly hydrated. Mountain biking is an endurance sport and requires plenty of energy, much of which is sourced from carbohydrates broken down to form glucose – the essential energy stored in the muscles.

Fruit, vegetables, breads, pastas, cereals, rice, and other starch and sugar-rich foods are all good sources of carbohydrates. Try to plan ahead of a big ride by eating carb-rich foods two or three days beforehand. Such 'carbo-loading' maximises the amount of glucose stored in your muscles, helping fuel a more sustained effort over a longer period.

It is also important to consume carbohydrates during longer rides to prevent muscles from becoming depleted. Energy bars, bananas and specialist carbohydrate drinks will all do the trick.

And keeping hydrated is no less important when mountain biking. Waiting until you feel thirsty is too late. Try instead to keep sipping as you ride. Becoming even slightly dehydrated impairs not only your performance, but also your reaction time, judgement and concentration – all vital functions when on the trail.

Remember that clothing can also influence the amount of fluid loss experienced. Heavy, non-wicking clothing interferes with sweat evaporation and can increase dehydration. Cotton, in particular, is rotten. Couple this with a decrease in body temperature on fast downhill sections due to wind chill and life can become quite uncomfortable. It is well worth investing in breathable clothing suitable for active sports.

Trail etiquette

Whether riding on purpose-built singletrack or enjoying natural trails out in the wilds, riders should always practise good trail etiquette. The International Mountain Bicycling Association's (IMBA) globally recognised rules include the concept of 'yielding' the trail. By yielding, the IMBA means 'slow down, communicate with the people you meet, be prepared to stop and pass safely'.

And this is particularly applicable at Glentress where some trails are shared with blue, red, and black run users, meaning that it is quite possible to come across riders with very different skill levels. If you do catch someone up, maintain a healthy distance - about eight bike lengths is about right - as the rider up ahead may stop suddenly or feel unduly pressured if you are breathing down their neck. Only pass when it is safe to do so and let the rider know that you are coming through.

Likewise, if you see someone on the trail that looks like they might need help, ask. It is the right thing to do and spreads good trail karma. After all, you may need similar help yourself one day.

It is also important to be aware of and respect other users. Not all trails are just for bikers - even at mountain bike centres. Give way to walkers and horse riders and make sure they know you are approaching. In the case of horses, it is best to dismount. When you meet other trail users, you represent the whole mountain biking community. Don't let us down.

And when on the trail, try to minimise skidding where possible. A lot of blood, sweat and tears - not to mention money - has gone into creating purpose-built trails for our enjoyment. Ride them like you built them yourself. Erosion caused by skidding costs a scary amount of money to repair.

Glentress is home to the Tweed Valley Bike Patrol, the UK's first volunteer mountain bike ranger scheme. As well as helping promote responsible enjoyment of the forest and its trails, the rangers are on hand to provide riders with emergency assistance, bike repair skills and plenty of trail advice.

Riding safety

Whatever the terrain and regardless of ability, all mountain biking carries an element of risk. A momentary lapse of concentration on even the most benign stretch of track can lead to a spill - sometimes with painful consequences.

As such, two pieces of safety gear we would insist anyone who swings a leg over a bike at Glentress must have would be a helmet and gloves (ideally full-finger).

A helmet should fit well and be less than four years old as after that the polystyrene shell starts to weaken. The date of manufacture is usually marked on the inside of the helmet.

If you do crash or drop your helmet then you should replace it immediately as significant impact can weaken the shell. Most helmet manufacturers offer a reduced cost crash replacement programme.

Gloves are also a good idea for grip, warmth and protection - particularly given how riders tend to instinctively put their hands out during a fall. There are loads of nerve endings in your hands, and particularly the fingers, so full-finger gloves are a must.

The use of other safety gear such as body armour is very much down to personal preference. Some riders wear it just for playing on Freeride areas, while others also use it on the trail. If you feel more confident and comfortable wearing body armour on the trail, then go for it - just be sure that it does not encourage you to ride beyond your limits.

grades

Trails are graded according to difficulty and the grading system below is generally recognised. In all cases, though, the weather, the quality of your bike and the ability of your companions can change the difficulty of a route.

Green easy: suitable for beginners and families on mountain bikes. Mostly level terrain with shallow climbs and descents on usually hardened surfaces but may be loose, uneven and muddy

Blue moderate: suitable for intermediate-level riders with basic off-road skills on mountain bikes. Moderate gradients, with possible short steep sections and obstacles such as rocks and roots

Red difficult: suitable for competent mountain bikers with good off-road skills on better-quality mountain bikes with recommended front suspension (forks). Steeper, tougher climbs and drops with berms, boardwalks, steps, large stones, possible water crossings and cambers. Varied surface 0.4m+ wide

Black severe: suitable for expert riders with a high level of fitness and stamina on good-quality mountain bikes with front suspension. Extended steep sections; large steps and drop-offs. Varied but always challenging surface with prolonged rocky/loose sections

Orange bikepark: suitable for expert riders aspiring to a high level of technical ability. Includes challenging constructed trail features, jumps and drops with high levels of exposure and risk.

First gear

Whether new to mountain biking and wanting to start off on the right track, or you have been riding for a while and are hungry for additional knowledge, then this chapter will help point you in the right direction.

It opens with some tips on bike selection before walking you through how best to position the saddle, handlebars, brake levers and other settings for your specific height, weight and anticipated riding.

This chapter also includes pointers on what to expect from different tyre pressures, plus a maintenance checklist that is well worth incorporating into your pre-ride routine. Such attention to detail will pay dividends in terms of riding comfort, safety and efficiency.

But while several entries in this chapter highlight specific rules of thumb when getting to grips with your mountain bike, much of what follows is a lot down to personal preference. Some riders are very specific about saddle height, pedal type and so on, but it is perhaps best not to get too bogged down in the fine detail to begin with. Just find what feels right for you and then make minor changes as you progress.

Likewise, how much you push yourself as you progress is also very much up to you, but this chapter and those that follow will equip you for what will hopefully be many years of enjoyment on the trail.

Choosing your mountain bike

With such a wide choice available, choosing the right mountain bike can be a daunting task

Much will depend on budget, of course, but be sure to also consider the kind of riding that you anticipate doing. If aiming to gradually progress your trailriding skills, you will need a bike that can cope with some of the demanding terrain and technical singletrack that you are likely to encounter.

Take your time, get some sound advice from a good independent bike shop and try a few models for size before taking the plunge. Your choice of bike will have a major impact on how you progress as a rider.

If new to the sport, we would always recommend purchasing a 'hardtail' - that is, one with no rear suspension. Not only are hardtails usually lighter and easier on the wallet, but they also help you get the basic skills right. Hardtails make riders really think about their riding and work a bit harder: this is important, as the habits you develop when you start riding are the ones that will stay with you as you progress to higher levels.

For those who have already taken the plunge and bought a bike with full suspension, do not despair. You have already done yourself a big favour by buying this book - it means you are open and willing to learn. It will also help iron out any bad habits you might already have developed.

Back in the day when we both raced professionally we lived next door to an older guy called Carl. He had been a prolific marathon runner and had decided to give mountain biking a go. He knocked on our door one night and presented his new pride and joy: a 21-inch full-suspension mountain bike. Now Carl stands at about 5ft six inches tall, which meant that the bike was at least five inches too big for him. It also weighed the equivalent of a small family car. We gently pointed this out, but he was determined to give mountain biking a shot. To his credit, Carl rode his new garden gate for a good while until we managed to persuade him to give one of our 16-inch hire bikes a ride. He has never looked back. Carl is now 66 years young and his enthusiasm for the sport sees him at Glentress almost every day in his role as chief mountain bike patroller.

Saddle height and rails

A correct saddle position is essential for ensuring a smooth, efficient ride

The first point to mention here is that saddle height and position are matters of personal preference. Some riders are very precise, finding that raising or lowering a saddle by just a couple of millimetres can make a big difference. Such riders often mark a preferred saddle position and then lower and raise it according to terrain.

Although most riders will not be quite so exacting, it is important to remember that saddle height has a direct impact on riding efficiency. A saddle that is too high will cause you to over stretch your legs, often 'toeing' the pedals around. Conversely, a saddle that is too low makes it impossible to achieve a full leg extension, resulting in crucial power being lost with each revolution of the wheels.

To obtain the correct saddle height, sit on the bike with one leg at the bottom of its stroke and the heel of the foot over the pedal spindle. Then adjust the seat so that this leg is straight.

Although less apparent, the relationship between the nose of the saddle and the pedals is almost as important as actual saddle height. A useful exercise is to sit on the bike with pedals level and the ball of the foot on the centre of each pedal. Look for a straight line from the knee to the centre of the pedal spindle - something that can be checked by dropping a plumb line from the knee. When the saddle is correctly positioned, the line should hang over the centre of the pedal spindle. If not, move the saddle back and forth on its rails until it does.

Every year as part of the British team training squad we would head to Spain for winter training camps. Training would be based on road riding and we would do long days in the saddle. Our bikes had been prepared by British team mechanics and we'd all been rigged up to various jigs to measure the optimum position to maximise our power output. After the first day's ride, we were rolling back into the hotel car park when mountain bike legend Tim Gould drew alongside me and suggested I lower my saddle a couple of millimetres 'just to see how it feels'. Not one to argue with a world champion, I got out my Allen key and dropped the post a couple of millimetres. The next day we headed out for another mile-crunching ride and I couldn't believe the difference. It just goes to show that if something feels right, then it probably is. **TB**

For obvious anatomical reasons, men and women tend to prefer slightly different saddle types. Women's saddles are more flared at the rear because their 'sit' bones are wider apart.

Handlebars and brake levers

Help absorb shock and reduce fatigue by ensuring the correct positioning of handlebars and brake levers

Finding the correct handlebar reach and 'feel' is usually something that is determined when first buying a bike. However, minor adjustments can still be made later, if needed.

The best way is to sit normally on the bike and draw an imaginary line from the shoulder down the body and along the arms. The angle between them should be about 45 degrees.

Remember, however, that the longer a handlebar stem the slower the turning speed of the bike - something that becomes really apparent when negotiating tight corners. It is all about control, so find what is most comfortable for your riding style.

Most trail bikes today come equipped with riser bars - handlebars that bow in the middle - rather than flat handlebars that are better suited to crosscountry racing. Such a bowed shape provides good control and encourages a more aggressive riding position (see pp50-51). Riser bars should be set so that they encourage a good attack position with elbows out.

Once happy with your handlebars, it is important to also ensure that the brake levers are positioned correctly. Ideally, there should be a straight line from the

shoulders to the fingers when covering the brakes. Twist the levers on the bars to achieve this. The reach should be set so that your index finger sits in the hook of the lever end - a position that will make the ride more efficient and less sapping on the hands and arms. Don't be afraid to move the levers in towards the centre of the bars to achieve this.

When I first started riding, I never thought too much about my bike set-up. I just jumped on the bike as it came and lacked the knowledge or understanding to adjust anything anyway. If you look at old pictures of me racing, you will notice that I brake with my middle finger and not my index finger. The reason was simple: the brake levers were always just that little bit too far away for me to reach with my index finger, so I adapted. It wasn't until I stopped racing and actually looked at my bike set-up that I realised it was possible to improve my position and performance by adjusting the lever reach. **EG**

Pedal power

With the option to be clipped in or use 'flats', there is more to pedals than meets the eye

Again, pedal choice is very much a matter of personal taste with some riders preferring to be clipped in - using special shoes that clip directly to the pedal - while others prefer traditional 'flats' that allow freedom of movement for the foot.

Both have their merits. Being clipped in encourages a positive pedalling motion with the pedals turning in consistent circles. Such a direct physical attachment to the bike also provides much better power transfer: while on bumpy terrain there is less chance of your feet leaving the pedals.

On the other hand, being clipped in can hide poor technique and may encourage a degree of laziness. In some cases, there is less manoeuvrability as the feet have only a restricted amount of movement. Exiting from the bike is also more difficult - a point that can inhibit some riders from really pushing their limits.

For skills days at Glentress, riders tend to get a lot more out of their time using flats rather than being clipped in. With flats, you really know that your feet are being used properly. Flats allow freedom to explore, provide better control and allow

you to develop skills. They positively encourage movement on the bike, while you can also use your feet for steering and even the occasional dab on the ground when needed.

On the other hand, flats are less efficient for pedalling - perhaps something to consider for long days in the saddle.

Every winter Tracy and I make ourselves ride flat pedals for a couple of months. For the first few weeks we hate it - our feet bounce off - but it makes us realise just how lazy we've become with our technique. Sticking with it really improves our riding when we go back to being clipped in. **EG**

Understanding tyre pressure

Being aware of the relationship between tyre pressure and trail conditions can make all the difference when it comes to grip

There is often much debate between riders about 'correct' tyre pressure, although most agree that it is better to run a slightly higher pressure in the back wheel than the front.

But while personal preferences ensure there are plenty of variables, there are some key points to factor into your thinking. Tyre pressure, after all, has a direct impact on ground resistance (and therefore speed) as well as grip.

Generally speaking, the more pressure in a tyre, the less grip it has. This becomes particularly apparent when conditions are either very wet and muddy or extremely dry and dusty. In both cases, consider letting out some air to bring more tyre into contact with the ground to increase grip. The same applies for steep climbs with loose rock.

On the flipside, under-inflated tyres do not corner well at speed and are also prone to 'pinch' punctures, where the inner tube is pinched between the tyre and the rim of the wheel.

As a rule, you should be able to get a good pinch out of each tyre when squeezing it, but it is worth experimenting to find out what works best for you. It is obviously impractical to keep stopping and adjusting the tyre pressure for every change of terrain, so try to find a happy medium when riding on mixed trails. And always carry a bike pump. After all, they are not just for mending punctures.

New tyres should last for some time, but check them at regular intervals. Loss of grip, frequent punctures and visible signs such as bald spots and wear on the sidewalls are all indicators that it is time for a replacement. But remember: tyres are directional so make sure they are fitted the right way around.

Pre-ride checks

Setting time aside for a pre-ride check of your bike is a wise start to any day on the trail

Our hire bikes at Glentress are given a full bolt check every time they are ridden, but occasionally things do come loose - an illustration of the amount of punishment that bikes take out on the trail.

A bike will talk to you - and it pays to listen. Your pre-ride checks should start with a simple drop test: place the chain onto the largest ring to remove chain slap. Pick the bike up and drop it, listening for any unusual sounds. These act as alarm bells and need to be investigated before setting off. Isolate the noise by dropping one end of the bike at a time. Then do a more detailed 'M' check tracing the line of an imaginary letter 'M' from the back of the bike to the front.

Start with the skewer (1) that secures the back wheel to the rear fork. This should be tight and face backwards so as not to snag on anything during the ride. Next, hold the rear wheel and check that the bearing cones are not loose (a problem indicated by movement sideways). Move up to the saddle (2) and check that the

seat clamp is tight and the saddle is secure on its rails. Do so by holding each end of the saddle and checking for movement.

Now, check the bottom bracket (3). Hold the crank arm (not the pedal) and try to move it away from the bike. If there is movement then the cranks may need tightening, or it may be a sign of wear and tear. Next, hold the pedals and see if there is any movement. Spin the pedals to ensure that they rotate freely.

Then check that the stem (4) is secure: stand in front of the bike with the wheel held between your legs and try to rotate the bars from side to side. There should be no movement. To check the headset, turn your bars to either side at a 90-degree angle and pull the front brake on. Place your fingers around the top headset cup and try to push the bike forwards and backwards. If there is any movement then the headset may need to be tightened.

Finally, ensure that the front skewer (5) is tight and also check the front wheel for loose cones as per the rear.

Performing this kind of 'M' check not only ensures that your bike is safe to ride, but can also save money in the long term as loose components wear much more quickly.

Trailside repairs

For the World Cup racer and the complete beginner alike, there is nothing more frustrating than having your ride cut short by some form of equipment failure (or 'mechanical').

At best, a mechanical is an inconvenience that may result in a long walk back to the trailhead, but in failing daylight and dropping temperatures it may be far more serious. Rather than relying on mobile phones to get you out of trouble - coverage on the hill and in forests can be patchy - it is far better to have some basic knowledge of how to get yourself back up and running, even if the solution is only temporary.

Whole books have been written on the subject of bike mechanics so we will not try to reinvent the wheel. Instead, this chapter will concentrate on simple trailside repairs that will help get you home when out on a long ride.

It opens with entries on two of the most common problems encountered: changing a flat and mending a broken chain. Neither should stop you in your tracks for long if you follow the step-by-step guides that follow.

We then look at perhaps the least exciting part of any day on the trail: cleaning and general preventative maintenance. It may not be everyone's idea of a good time, but a thorough cleaning regime can extend the life of your bike significantly and also has a safety benefit. Close inspection of your bike can help pinpoint nuts and bolts that have come loose and other potential hazards.

Finally, we offer some imaginative solutions for when things go badly wrong, including creative uses for gaffa tape, toothpaste tubes and other items that are well worth packing with your regular toolkit.

Further reading

Recommended book: Big Blue Book of Bicycle Repair, C. Calvin Jones
Recommended website: sheldonbrown.com

Changing a flat

**Changing a flat is one of the most important skills to learn
- particularly if planning to ride far from home**

Some riders are lucky and hardly ever get a puncture, while others are less fortunate. One thing is for sure: punctures from thorns, heavy riding and even just worn-out tyres can happen at any time - often when furthest from home. However, with a few tips, changing a flat is straightforward and stress-free.

Removing the wheel. It is quicker to remove the punctured wheel with the bike the right way up rather than on its saddle. Hold the bike by the top tube so that you have a firm grip when you remove whichever wheel has punctured. If the flat is on the rear wheel, shift the rear derailleur to the smallest (hardest) cog on the back sprocket to relieve tension and make it easier to remove. Undo v-brakes by pushing the lever arms together and disconnecting the cable from its cradle. No adjustment is needed for disc brakes. If the bike has quick release skewers, pull the skewer outwards so that the wheel can be pulled from the frame. (If the flat is on the front wheel, you will need to unwind the skewer a bit more as the forks on the front have small lips to prevent the wheel popping out if the skewer accidentally comes loose.) For bikes with a solid axle, use an adjustable spanner (usually 15mm) to release the wheel.

Removing the tube. Fully deflate the inner tube. Hold the tyre with both hands and push it away from the rim all round the wheel. 'Debeading' the tyre in this way makes it much easier to remove. Now peel the bead off the rim using two or three tyre levers. Don't use anything sharp as you might cause another puncture. Take hold of the inner tube opposite the valve hole and pull from the inside of the tyre, finishing with the valve itself. Some tubes have a locking nut on the thread of the valve that needs to be removed for the valve to pass through the rim.

Finding and fixing the puncture. To find the puncture, keep the tube next to the wheel as it came out and inflate to locate the hole. Once located, line the tube up with the wheel and remove the offending object. You might even have two holes in the tube (a snakebite puncture), which is caused by the inner tube coming into heavy contact with the rim. Apply the repair patch according to the instructions on your puncture repair kit, although for speed it is best just to insert a new tube and save the actual repair for when back at home.

Refitting the wheel. Once ready, part-inflate the new (or repaired) tube to give it some shape. Re-insert the valve and push the tube back onto the rim, using your thumbs to work your way around the tyre until opposite the valve. Do not use tyre levers for this as they could easily pinch the tube. Once done, inflate the tyre to the desired pressure, although check to ensure that it is seated evenly on the rim halfway through inflation.

Replace the wheel, reattach the brakes and doublecheck that the wheel rotates and the chain is on properly (if mending the rear wheel). Now get back on the trail.

Placing the chain on the smallest cog when changing a rear wheel puncture also makes it easier to put the wheel back into the frame. This is because you automatically know that the chain has to be placed on the smallest cog, with no tension to fight against it.

Mending a broken chain

A broken chain sounds catastrophic, but need not mean the end of your ride

If you're unfortunate enough to suffer a chain break, then the damaged link needs to be removed and replaced or the chain rejoined. For this you will need a chain splitter - the only tool with which it is possible to rejoin a broken chain.

Often when a chain breaks, you will need to lose a link. This is because the break will have caused one of the links to twist, rendering it useless. Try not to lose too many links, however, as this will shorten the chain and adversely affect gear selection.

Preparation. Shift the gears to the smallest cog on the rear sprocket and slip the chain off the cogs on the front so it rests on the frame. This will allow you to work on the chain without it being under so much tension. Inspect the chain where it has split and decide where you want to rejoin it. By looking at the chain you will see that there is a natural fit that clips together to make the chain complete again.

Splitting the chain. Split the chain to the nearest link after the damaged part by placing the roller part of the chain in the chain tool. Turn the handle of the chain tool clockwise so the pin comes into contact with the rivet in the chain. If possible, work from behind the chain so that the rivet is pushed towards you as you face the bike. This will make life easier when you rejoin it.

Pushing the rivet. The aim now is to push the rivet out of the chain, but not so far that it falls out the other side; this is important because you need to push the rivet back into the chain to allow you to rejoin it. If the rivet is pushed all the way out then there is no way to get it back in and you will need to lose another link which will only make the chain even shorter.

Once the rivet is in this position, back out the chain tool pin, lift the chain out of the tool and remove the damaged link. It should come out with a little effort. If not, push the rivet a little further out, but be careful for the reason outlined above.

Once the damaged link has been removed, take the other end of the chain and put the two parts together. The small part of the rivet that is still in place should help them marry up. Make sure that the chain is threaded through the drive train correctly before you rejoin it.

Rejoining the chain. Now you are ready to rejoin the chain. Place the chain in the tool again as before with the pin wound out. Once happy with the position of the chain in the tool, turn the handle clockwise until the pin meets the rivet and starts to push through the centre of the chain. Gently force the rivet through, making sure the links and pin remain central. Push the rivet through until it is in the centre of the links and back out the chain tool pin.

Remove the chain from the tool and take hold of the chain either side of the join and flex it gently back and forward. This helps the chain to settle into position and ensures that you don't end up with a stiff link that can cause the gears to jump as the chain passes through the rear gear. Check this by moving the chain up and down - it should move freely. If not, flex again gently from side to side.

An alternative to rejoining what becomes a shortened chain is to carry Powerlinks instead. Powerlinks work by joining each end of the chain at the inner link. The advantage is that you will not need to stress about pushing the rivet to the exact position, as the rivet is part of the Powerlink. These 'missing links' come in 8-speed or 9-speed so make sure you carry the right one for your bike.

Cleaning and maintenance

Keeping on top of cleaning and maintenance not only makes your bike look good but can also save money in the long run

To keep your bike really clean, you will need a good set of brushes - ideally a soft one for the frame and a stiffer, thinner brush for the drive chain - plus some old rags for drying. Use a bike cleaner such as Hope Sh*t Shifter or Muc-Off for cleaning the frame and forks, plus a degreaser, such as Finish Line eco-tech for the moving parts. All are biodegradable and wash off easily with water.

Be systematic. First, rinse any excess mud or grit from the bike with a hose. Try not to use a power hose as the force of the water can drive the essential layer of grease from the bike's moving parts. Start from the top and work down, washing away all signs of mud and grit so that it will not be worked into the frame when using the brush.

If planning to degrease the chain and cogs, then do this first using the stiff brush or a chain cleaner if you have one.

Work the degreaser into the cogs and chain, allowing it to soak in and really loosen the excess grease and oil (although take care not to get it into the hubs or headset).

Rinse the degreaser off gently with the hose until the water runs clear, moving the chain round as you rinse.

Next, wet a soft brush and spray it with bike cleaner. Again, start from the top of the bike and work down over the frame and forks. Leave the wheels and spokes/discs to last as you are likely to pick up bits of dirt that can scratch the frame.

Be thorough. Think about where dirt collects as you ride; all too often, the underside of the brake levers, beneath the seat and the undercarriage of the bike are missed. Leave the bike cleaner for a couple of minutes, then rinse off with a gentle stream of water.

Polishing your bike will leave a protective film over the frame and forks that will make washing easier next time. However, when spraying polish and lube take care not to spray the disc pads or brake rims, as this will seriously affect your brakes. It is best to spray the polish onto a clean rag rather than directly onto the bike.

Drying and lubing. Once rinsed, wrap a clean rag around the chain and turn the pedals backwards until the chain is dry (best done with the chain in the middle gears). Give the frame a final wipe over with another clean rag to remove any excess water.

Once the bike is clean, it is important to lubricate the chain and cogs using either dry lube or wet lube. Dry lube goes on wet but dries to a pasty film that repels grit and grime. It is ideal for dry, dusty conditions,

but will still protect your chain in wet weather. Although it usually needs re-applying after each ride, one advantage is that the chain will not become excessively oily.

Wet lube, on the other hand, is ideal for wet weather, long-distance riding. It goes on wet and stays that way. However, be careful not to over apply: wet lube can attract dirt and grime producing a grinding paste that can wear down components at an alarming rate.

Creative repairs

Sometimes a little imagination and creativity is required to get you out of trouble while on the trail

Despite regular maintenance and cleaning, there will be times when something fails on your bike.

Be prepared and carry tools that are relevant to your bike and where you are riding. Having a 'mechanical' far from home is no fun at all. Not being able to do anything about it is even worse.

So, in addition to the usual kit, it is well worth packing the following:

• Tyre boot in case of tyre rip. Old toothpaste tubes work well – just trim the sharp edges off
• Gaffa tape
• Zip ties - different sizes
• A few spare bolts specific to your bike
• Extra gear cable
• Multi-tool that includes pliers and knife
• Spare gear hanger
• Small bottle of lube for those annoying little squeaks
• Coach bolt

Here are some creative solutions for common trail emergencies:

Rip in sidewall of tyre. This can be caused by a rock slashing the tyre, or v-brakes rubbing on a sidewall. Deflate the tyre and place the tyre boot or old toothpaste tube over the slash/hole.

Twisted chain. A chain can become twisted if it has jammed against the frame or been forced through a bad gear change. Although difficult, try to straighten it using pliers (and then replace the chain as soon as possible).

Bent/broken gear hanger. This can happen when the rear gear hits a rock or even by laying the bike down on the gears. Carrying a spare gear hanger is a good idea. Hangers are made from soft metal and are designed to bend and break to prevent damage to the frame. If you do not have a spare hanger, try to bend it back - but be gentle.

Other options. If you don't have a spare hangar then you will need to convert the bike to a single-speed to at least get you

Remember when you make an emergency repair it is probably temporary - see it as your get-out-of-jail-free card. Don't jump on your bike and start hammering down the hill. Take it easy otherwise you may face an even bigger problem.

home. To do this, remove the rear gear first by breaking the chain, then unbolting the gear and what is left of the hanger from the frame. Select a gear that is suitable to the terrain you are riding (uphill is the biggest consideration as you can always coast downhill).

Rejoin the chain as tightly as you can, otherwise it will keep falling off. In fact, it may still do so - it is impossible to get the chain very taut on a bike designed for gears - but do the best you can.

If it keeps falling off, it's time to get really creative. It is possible to use zip ties, gaffa tape and toothpaste wrapper to cobble together a makeshift cradle that will hold the chain a bit tighter.

Loose pedal. Tighten it if you have a tool. Continuous riding on a loose pedal is likely to strip the thread and render the crank unusable. Another option is to carry a coach bolt with the large, square end filed down so it fits through the crank arm. The nut can then be tightened against the arm of the crank - just enough to get you home without having to walk.

The basics

Trailriding is often instinctive, but as the best riders will testify, that instinct also needs to be backed up with technique - something that is often forgotten when the adrenaline begins to flow.

As such, this chapter begins very much at the beginning, taking a back to basics approach to the core skills that underpin most aspects of trailriding. It offers an important reminder of the fundamental techniques required for progress. Ignore these, and your riding will always hit a plateau. Take them on board - and practise them consistently - and you will have a foundation for

almost unlimited development as a rider.

This section opens with an explanation of two techniques that are central to everything that you will subsequently do on a mountain bike: the cone of movement and weight transfer. It then breaks down skills that many riders perhaps take for granted, such as looking ahead, efficient gearing and the mechanics of braking.

Avoid the temptation to rush through this chapter to get to the sexier stuff: it will serve you well - and quite possibly save you some bumps and bruises along the way.

Cone of movement

The greater your 'cone of movement', the better your control when riding - and that means standing rather than sitting

The more freedom of movement you have on a mountain bike the better. That is why one of the most important points to understand when starting out is the concept of a 'cone of movement'.

When sitting, a rider has only a limited cone of movement as the cone effectively starts at the body's contact point - in this case, your backside on the saddle. This is okay when riding along even trails, but is no good for when the terrain becomes bumpier. Sitting down provides very little reaction time or control - a crash waiting to happen when obstacles come thick and fast.

Standing in what is known as the 'attack' position, however, opens up a whole new world of balance and movement. As soon as you stand tall on the bike, the amount of movement is increased as the cone now starts at the pedals. A rider can twist and turn with much greater balance while still maintaining control of the bike.

Try it. A correct attack position sees roughly a 60/40 weight distribution - with 60 to the front and 40 to the back - a relaxed grip on the bars, arms and legs slightly bent, feet level on the pedals for an even distribution of weight and head looking up to anticipate what is coming next. In this position you are ready for anything the trail has to offer. Practise moving around on the bike, bringing your body weight over the handlebars and behind the saddle - you will be amazed at how much movement is possible.

Think of the saddle as a reference point that tells you where you are on the bike, not a comfy seat. Riders should stand as much as possible, even on bikes equipped with full suspension.

When the Spooky Wood was first built (cheers Richard) it really pushed the envelope of trail centre riding in the UK and challenged how people rode their bikes. There used to be a bit of tradition that you never lowered your seat post on a crosscountry bike; to do so was seen in some quarters as sacrilege. With the evolution of trails like Spooky, it's become really important to lower your post so that you can move around the bike and control it better - and, of course, more movement means way more fun.

Perfecting weight transfer

Mastering good forward and backward movement is key to becoming a smoother rider

We all naturally move up and down on our bikes when riding, but it is the movement or weight transfer forward and backward that really encourages smoothness and control.

A good way to perfect this is to practise on a trail that includes one or a series of medium-sized humps. Tackling the hump at a steady speed demonstrates the mechanics of weight transfer. Much like walking up a hill, your weight naturally leans forward and then levels out as you reach the brow. And as the ground and bike level out, your weight naturally returns to the attack position so that you are ready for the next obstacle. Imagine trying to stay upright, but with the bike essentially moving through your body.

Try it. Approach the hump in the attack position with your legs at the same angle (i.e. pedals level). As you ride up the hump, your weight should naturally shift forward before becoming neutral at the top of the hump and then shift back over the saddle to compensate as you ride down the other side. On the way down, do not shift your weight too far back on the bike - let the terrain dictate how much you should move the bike through you. Such a transfer means that your weight is always central to the position of the bike, which in turn ensures good grip (traction) with both wheels.

Be strict with yourself initially so you can really perfect moving the bike through you. Stay tall and relaxed, and try to avoid too much bend in your arms.

Using natural suspension

Once comfortable with moving forwards and back, it is time to reintroduce up and down movement to maximise control and grip

Up and down movement, or crouching, on your bike achieves two things: it acts as natural suspension as you negotiate specific terrain and offers better grip on the trail when applied at the right time.

Imagine standing on your bathroom scales with arms and legs straight, then quickly bending and dropping your bum towards your heels. For a split second, your weight increases. Do this on a bike and both weight and grip increase.

It is crucial that you combine this crouching movement with good weight shift forward and back as without it you will be unweighting the bike in the wrong places.

Try it. Using the same hump as in the previous weight transfer exercise, this time crouch down in addition to moving your weight forward as you ride up the slope. Bring your bike through your body as you crest, pushing the bike down the far side of the hump.

This takes a bit of getting used to, so start with just your arms, allowing the bike to come towards you on the up slope, then pushing the bars down the far side. Once comfortable with this and you are in tune with the terrain, introduce your legs and do the same thing. Think of a skier absorbing moguls, but all the while pushing the skis downwards to maintain contact with the slope.

Looking ahead

Looking down the trail and anticipating what is coming next is a much underused skill

Often, what separates the better riders from the average ones is something very simple: looking ahead. Riders that make negotiating particular obstacles look easy do so because they have assessed what is needed long before they actually reach them. Such riders look ahead and anticipate rather than just reacting blindly.

Of course, looking ahead rather than at your front wheel also aids stability - and safety. If you look at an obstacle, that is where you will go. Those rocks aren't magnetic, although it can sometimes seem that way.

At purpose-built centres such as Glentress, the concept of looking ahead and seeing the start and finish of obstacles can be practised on balance beams or short sections of North Shore (raised timber trail) in the skills areas.

Try it. As you approach, look ahead to the start of the balance beam and note your point of entry. Once on the beam, look ahead to the next reference point - either the middle or end depending on the length of the obstacle. Don't look down directly ahead of your front wheel as this will only make you unstable. Instead, try to freeze frame the beam, breaking it down into sections. Be sure to also assess your exit point. If the beam is just a few inches off the ground then it will be like plopping off a kerb if you come off the side, so there is no reason to panic.

Looking ahead also helps with general trailriding and can be applied to all situations - particularly cornering.

Practise your skills to give you the confidence to try higher obstacles, but build up gradually and be consistent. That way you will know that you have the necessary skills to tackle the scarier stuff.

When I was racing on the World Cup xc circuit I always found I would lose my mojo on the last lap and negotiating obstacles that I had ridden over in previous laps would become a real challenge. At first I put it down to tiredness, but when I really thought about it I realised that although fatigue was part of it, I had started to drop my head and look down and this was making me less smooth over technical terrain. To combat this I placed a bright orange sticker on my stem so that whenever it crept more directly into my line of vision it reminded me to look ahead. **TB**

The art of braking

Understanding the physics of braking will give you more stopping power, control and confidence

Learning how to brake correctly involves understanding the relative effectiveness of the front and rear brakes. If riding a trail using either just the front brake or just the rear, it will quickly become apparent which brake provides the most control: the front brake wins every time.

So, throw out a notion from childhood that the front brake should be avoided. True, if you slam on the front anchors too hard, you will take a trip over the handlebars. This is because the front brake has 70% stopping power against 30% at the back. Riders should keep this ratio in mind when braking.

The trick is to feather rather than snatch both front and back brakes together when coming to a stop. To do so effectively, however, it is important to know the biting point of each. This is the point at which the brake pads come into contact with the rim or rotor and you start to scrub speed. Of course, the harder the lever is pulled, the more dramatic the effect.

Try it If your bike has hydraulic disc brakes then it is possible to use just one finger to brake - the most efficient, and strongest, being the index finger. Using the index finger means that the rest of the hand remains on the handlebars ensuring both stopping power and control. Using just one finger also sends a clear message to your brain - far better when having to think fast.

In addition, looking ahead and anticipating the braking required allows you to get your weight in the right position on the bike. If you intend to brake hard, say before a corner, remember to lean back a little as pulling the brakes will cause your body weight to transfer forward. Doing this will ensure your weight is where it should be, with good traction on the front wheel.

Trail design has come a long way since the first tracks were built in Glentress. Not only do the newer trails give you a massive buzz but they allow new riders to experience the thrill of mountain biking without being terrified the first time on a bike. If you ride *Blue Velvet*, for example, you don't have to brake too much because after each downhill you are always run back up a slope to scrub off your speed. This keeps the rider safe because braking efficiently at speed is a hard skill to master, and it keeps the trailbuilder happy because fewer skids mean less erosion.

Effective gearing

Anticipating the gear required for each section of trail helps to preserve energy on the uphill and maintain control on the downhill

Gears are often referred to as 'high' or 'low', but we prefer 'easy' or 'hard'. The left shifter on the handlebars controls the front chain rings. There are normally three: the smallest (and easiest), a middle ring (the one most often used) and the largest (or hardest).

The right shifter controls the rear gears and are either eight- or nine-speed. Usually, pushing with the thumb makes it harder, while clicking with the finger makes it easier.

It is always best to choose a gear that allows ease of movement, but not one that is spinning out uncontrollably. Too high a cadence is a sure way of tiring yourself out unnecessarily.

Do not be afraid to change gear a lot, particularly on terrain that often requires minor adjustments along the way.

Try it. Try riding the same section of trail using different gears to see what feels comfortable. Also, practise anticipating the gear required for particular sections of trail. It is also best to avoid changing gear when it is too late: trying to change gear on a steep uphill section puts immense pressure on the drivetrain and can cause gears to jump, losing you crucial momentum.

When riding, think carefully about your chain line - the relationship between the front and rear cogs. Avoid big/big and small/small. Instead, try to keep the chain in a straight line, for example, on the middle ring at the front and on the third or fourth ring at the rear.

Essential skills

Now that you have the core techniques in place it is time to add a layer of skills that will allow you to tackle many of the common obstacles found on the trail. Again, we keep things simple and encourage you to build your skills gradually, only moving on to the harder stuff once you have gained sufficient confidence in your ability.

The skills covered in this chapter will really make you think about your riding and how the application of weight transfer and carefully applied power will help you negotiate particular sections of trail.

This chapter opens with three entries on cornering, starting with looking ahead on easier corners before examining the techniques required to sweep around tighter sections with fluent ease.

We then cover specific skills that could be used a hundred times on the average ride – or even more if actively seeking suitable obstacles. Once mastered, the manual and power-assisted front wheel lifts will give you the technical ability to approach all but the toughest of obstacles with supreme confidence.

Finally, we end by exploring how best to get up - and down - even the steepest terrain using many of the core skills learnt in previous chapters.

Look and attack

Successful cornering is all about looking, leaning and leading with the body

Every rider dreams of sweeping around corners with fluent ease, but it is a skill that takes time to really master – with looking ahead the key.

As outlined in the previous chapter (p40), you should be looking several metres ahead and trying to 'freeze frame' the corner into the approach, middle and exit point. Pick out a stone, clump of grass, or anything that will act as a marker and help guide your eye around the corner. As you become used to this technique, you will find yourself freeze framing that much faster until you are scanning the trail almost effortlessly.

However, be sure to maintain your attack position when cornering. It is common for riders to sit when corners become challenging as it feels safer to be closer to the ground. All this does is reduce your cone of movement and control of the bike. It also moves all of your weight to the back, putting little weight and, therefore, grip on the front wheel at a time when it is needed most.

Try it. Start several metres before a wide, smooth corner and pedal with sufficient momentum to get into the attack position well before you enter the corner. As you approach, fix your eyes on a point about a third of the way into the corner. As you reach that initial reference point, lift your eyes to the next point – ideally the centre, or just beyond the centre of the corner. Again, don't fixate on this point, but look quickly instead to the exit and beyond. By looking around the corner in this way, your shoulders will naturally twist in the direction you are heading. And when looking more aggressively, such as on a tighter corner, your hips will also begin to twist all the way down to the feet. Such body rotation effectively helps your bike around each corner.

Visual skills need honing as much as any other skill - particularly for riders new to mountain biking. Try to slow down to give yourself more time to perfect this crucial technique, ideally using a smooth corner that allows you to concentrate on technique without worrying about obstacles. Once you've mastered the technique then you can start to add speed.

Squashing the 'O'

Now load the front wheel with extra weight for faster, more confident cornering

Once comfortable with looking around a corner in the attack position, you will soon be able to add speed. This is when you need to introduce additional skills that will allow you to tackle more tricky corners with confidence.

As you get faster, it is important to increase the grip on the front wheel in the middle, or apex, of the corner - the point where you need it most. To do this, you need to load the front wheel with extra weight.

Try it. When in the attack position, think of the upper body formation as a letter 'O'. As you enter the corner, you need to gradually start to squash that O shape by bringing your chest down towards the bars - with the O squashed the most at the apex of the corner. Allow your legs to relax and bend into the apex of the corner. As you exit the corner, start to come back up again and return to the original attack position. You can accentuate this by leading with your elbow, bringing your body weight forward and providing maximum grip on the front wheel. Of course, the faster you travel, the more grip you need on that front wheel, so the more weight (and, therefore, lean) is required. The weight then comes off as you exit the corner.

Ski cornering

Skiers will recognise the technique required for tackling tighter corners

Descending through tight hairpins
takes cornering to another level and can
be wonderfully satisfying when
performed correctly. Here more than
ever, however, fluidity is key.

The secret to tackling tighter downhill
corners lies in transferring weight to your
outer foot and pushing into the pedal as
you corner. On a right-hand corner, for
instance, push down hard on your left pedal
and lean into the turn. Think of it like skiing,
where extra pressure is exerted on the outer
ski, while the inside ski – or, in this case, the
inside pedal – is lifted to just lightly graze
the snow.

Try it. First get your speed right: brake comfortably before the corner, not as you enter it. Remember to look ahead, then lift the inside pedal. This will naturally put all your weight on the outside pedal - like standing on one leg - and encourage you to lean into the corner. Be careful, though: if the pedals are not positioned correctly, it is all too easy to hit the ground - with potentially unfortunate results.

Bermed corners - those with banking that hold you onto the trail - provide a perfect opportunity to practise cornering technique. Just remember that the grip comes from the banking so that is where you need to apply pressure. Lean with the bike, push through the outer pedal into the banking and accelerate through the corner.

Weighting

Improve control of your bike by keeping on the move

You should now be starting to understand how moving around your bike and transferring your weight can help maximise and influence the control and grip you have. It's logical if you think about it: your weight is at least twice that of the bike, so shifting your weight whilst holding the bike will affect its course and direction.

Unweighting either end of the bike is the first step in understanding how to control the bike over trail obstacles like roots and rocks. Practise with small obstacles - rocks, roots, kerbs - to improve your technique. Once you've got the hang of it over a single obstacle, start to apply it more than once in a section of trail and you will soon be able to smooth out whatever the trail throws at you.

Try It. Approach the obstacle, starting with a small root or rock step that you can coast towards in the attack position. Just before the front wheel reaches the obstacle, move your weight towards the rear of the bike by shifting your hips backwards and straightening your arms. This action of loading your weight towards the back of the bike unweights the front wheel as it rolls over the obstacle. When the front wheel is over, move your hips towards the bars so the rear of the bike becomes unweighted and easily rolls over the roots or rock. Once clear of the obstacle return to the attack position.

This skill can also save you money. If you keep puncturing on the rear, then it is possible you are leaving your weight at the back of the bike too much: by shifting your weight forward over obstacles you will go lighter on your tyre and rim.

Manual front wheel lift

Avoid obstacles with ease using weight transfer rather than brute force

A manual front wheel lift takes the skill of weighting and unweighting one step further. By being more dramatic in your movement - but using essentially the same concept - you can start to tackle larger trail obstacles.

A great skill, best utilised at reasonable speed on flat ground or while descending, the manual allows you to smooth the trail by lifting the front wheel clear of rocks, roots and other minor obstacles.

The key here, however, is to lift the front wheel by transferring your weight rather than trying to lift it with your arms.

Try it. Approach the obstacle - start with just a stick laid on the trail - in the attack position. Just before reaching the obstacle, rock your body forward (moving your hips towards the bars) with straight but relaxed arms and legs and then explode backwards by throwing your shoulders towards the back of the bike. This is done with a straight body that pivots from the feet. Try not to bend your arms as this brings the shoulders forward and weight down on the front wheel making it that much harder to gain lift. The same applies to the head: look beyond the obstacle you are trying to avoid, not down at the front wheel. Hold your body weight for a split second at the end of the weight shift and then rock forwards into your starting position.

As you improve and are able to lift the front wheel higher, start to also drop your heels to give added acceleration by pushing the bike underneath you. Remember to always cover the back brake in case you go back too far: a quick dab will bring the front wheel down immediately.

Power-assisted front wheel lift

**Lifting the front wheel using a power stroke can help propel
your bike over tricky obstacles when climbing**

Sometimes when climbing at slower speed, you will not have enough momentum to get the bike over rock steps and other more technical difficulties using just a manual lift. Instead, such obstacles require a power-assisted front wheel lift – a smooth power stroke combined with a backward movement of the body to create explosive, but controlled lift.

The secret here, as ever, lies in balance and correct weight shift. Pedalling in the saddle at an easy walking pace, crouch forward towards the bars by bending your arms. As your lead foot rolls over the top of the stroke – the 12 o'clock position – fix your eyes on something ahead in the distance. Then as you near the one o'clock position, increase the power through the stroke while throwing your shoulders to the back of the bike, straightening your arms and pushing your lead leg downwards to six o'clock. All three actions must happen smoothly and at the same time for a successful move.

Try it. Initially practise without any obstacles and build from there. Be sure to keep your arms straight and your weight back. If you throw your weight back with enough commitment then you will find your balance point; this is a good thing as it means you are becoming familiar with your range of movement for this skill. If you feel like you are going to fall backwards then apply the rear brake a little to bring the front wheel down.

Be sure to choose the right gear for what is very much a slow speed skill. Too easy a gear and there will be insufficient power to lift the front wheel; too hard a gear and it will be impossible to push the power down – a bit like trying to drive off in a car in third gear.

Climbing best practice

A combination of anticipation, rhythm and good body position will take some of the pain out of long climbs

The mountain biking gods decree that for every thrilling downhill, there must first be a potentially gruelling uphill. It's a fair trade-off given the sheer enjoyment of hurtling downhill – although a successful climb can also be immensely satisfying.

Correct gearing (see p58) plays a huge part here, but so too does simple anticipation. Look ahead, get a feel for the terrain and anticipate what is coming next.

Is the climb short and steep, or is it a long, sustained gradient? Whatever the challenge, try to pace yourself carefully. There is no point burning out before the end of the ascent.

Climbing can also be made more comfortable - and efficient - by shifting your weight towards the front of the bike. The use of your torso in this way adds weight (and, therefore, grip) to the front

On very steep or more technical sections it will be necessary to stand rather than sit. In such cases, use your body weight to power the pedals, but keep your core torso still. It is the bike that should move to the left and right, not your body.

wheel, while still leaving the rear wheel with plenty of traction. It also allows a good transfer of power with each stroke, reducing the chance of rear wheel spin.

Finally, such a position encourages you to pull back on the bars and push forward with your feet - so enabling you to pedal in circles rather than stomping vertically down on the pedals with your feet.

Try it. When climbing, remain seated and twist your wrists as if revving a motorbike. This has the affect of bringing your elbows in and pulling your shoulders down to the front of the bike. As the trail becomes steeper, gradually shift your core weight to the front of the saddle. Try to conserve energy and leave one or two easier gear settings in reserve should you need them for the final push.

Downhill best practice

Downhill sections provide a perfect opportunity to practise many of the core skills covered within this chapter

Most riders agree, downhill is where the real fun is - a fine reward for any climbs that came before. All too often, however, the temptation is just to bomb headlong down the trail, essentially surviving each obstacle rather than applying specific skills. As a result, riders arrive at the bottom exhilarated, but also somewhat amazed that they have made it in one piece.

While enormous fun, downhill sections should also be seen as an opportunity to put together many of the core skills covered in this chapter. Understanding and applying these skills will enable you to go both faster and safer, with the confidence to cope with whatever is around the next corner.

Try it. Before pitching yourself down the trail, think carefully about what you have learnt - and what may be coming. Choose a gear in advance that gives good tension in the chain and will allow you to pedal out of trouble if needed. The middle ring is best. Stand tall in the attack position with a good cone of movement, ready to manoeuvre around obstacles. Look ahead, keep to a controllable speed and be ready to feather the brakes when necessary. Above all, relax, focus and enjoy the ride.

It sounds counter-intuitive, but to go faster, you must slow down. Think about where you are on the trail and where you want to be next. Mountain biking is like a game of pool in that each move is designed to set you up for the next one.

When I first met Tracy she was racing crosscountry and I was racing downhill. She would tease me that downhillers were a bit crazy and that we all took our brains out (if we had any) at the top of the hill. That was until she was contracted to race some of the World Cup downhills by the American team she was riding for. After that she realised that not only do you need more skill but also more brainpower to go downhill - everything is coming at you super fast and you need to be able to think and make decisions very quickly - if I hadn't have raced downhill I'm sure the field of quantum physics would have beckoned. *EG*

Theory into practice

Now it is time to apply the skills learnt in preceding chapters to very specific obstacles out on the trail. Some are benign and can be tackled with ease. Others are more serious and require courage and commitment, as well as technique.

This chapter opens with three entries examining various drop-offs and rolls – familiar obstacles for regulars at Glentress. The trick with all such obstacles is to start small and build up as you gradually hone your skills. Try not to take on too much, too soon.

We then devote two entries to jumping,

a skill that may seem quite advanced but is nonetheless well within the reach of even novice riders. Again, it is best to start small and work up, always scoping out larger obstacles in advance before attempting to ride them. Such preparation can make all the difference between a successful manoeuvre and a nasty spill.

Finally, we end with two entries that help you put all the jigsaw pieces together: one that helps you break tricky sections down into bite-size portions and the other that shows how to create the perfect flow out on the trail.

The safe roll

Smaller drop-offs can be tackled using a controlled roll rather than any kind of jump

The safe roll is perhaps the most controlled way to tackle smaller drop-offs of up to a foot or so. However, a safe roll is only an option when it is possible for the front wheel to touch the lower level before the rear wheel of the bike leaves the edge. Assessing the extent of the drop is essential.

And there are some other golden rules to follow. First, your cone of movement is crucial for this skill, so lower your saddle a little to allow more movement around the bike. Also think carefully about where your weight should be: some weight shift is required, but do not be tempted to push your weight right to the back of the bike as this will unweight the front leaving you with little control.

Try it. As you approach the drop, look ahead and decide whether it can be rolled. Make your decision and then keep the bike moving at a steady speed - do not brake. If you are not going to commit, stop now. Just before you leave the edge, make sure your weight is in the middle of the bike in the attack position so that you have good control of the front end of the bike. Let the nose of the bike drop and shift your weight

towards the back of the bike as the roll dictates. Let the rear wheel follow through smoothly. You will feel at your most vulnerable as the rear wheel leaves the edge, but it's too late to turn back now. Just look ahead and hold your line. Let the rear wheel drop to the lower level and stay relaxed. When the rear wheel clears the roll, come back to a neutral position and keep looking ahead.

If you picked up more speed than you wanted on approach, look ahead to identify good areas to brake after you have cleared the drop/roll.

Larger drop-offs

Larger drop-offs are a real confidence tester, but with commitment can be negotiated with ease

When a drop-off is of sufficient size that the front wheel does not touch down before the rear wheel leaves the edge, a little more energy and commitment is required to guarantee a safe landing.

A common mistake when approaching larger drop-offs is for riders to lift the front wheel just before 'take-off'. But doing so only serves to encourage more height on the front, forcing the rear wheel to land first. It also leaves a good chunk of your weight at the rear of the bike. Not good.

The skill required for larger drop-offs relies on a weight transfer that comes from the bike rather than the rider - in other words, an acceleration of the bike forward that in turn shifts the rider back. When performed with sufficient forward momentum, both wheels land together. If not, the front wheel lands while the rear wheel remains on top of the obstacle, turning the move into an unstable version of the roll-off technique detailed earlier.

Try it. Find a drop-off that steps down only a matter of inches, such as a curb. Approach the obstacle in the attack position. Bend your arms and legs slightly and crouch towards the front of the bike. As the front wheel reaches the edge, push (not lift) the bike forward with your hands and feet – a move that accelerates the bike forward and shifts your weight back. Such

momentum, plus looking ahead and spotting your landing, will enable both wheels to either land together, or the front slightly before the rear. When the bike lands it naturally slows because of the friction, so bringing you back to the attack position. Once you can consistently clear both wheels and land smoothly, you are ready to tackle larger drop-offs.

If you find yourself landing on the rear wheel, try to visualise pushing the bike forward and down to the landing slope.

The steep roll

Steep rolls can freak out even experienced riders, but there are ways to keep the nerves at bay

Steep rolls require commitment and courage. As such, when encountering this kind of obstacle for the first time it pays to look before you ride and ask yourself several questions. First, study the approach. What is the surface like? Is it a good, smooth surface that your wheels can roll over easily? Also, what speed is required to ensure a trouble-free entry onto the roll?

Then check out the exit. Is there a good transition at the point where the roll finishes and the trail resumes? Also, check that your wheel won't be caught and stutter momentarily on the exit. Finally, have a good look at the surface of the roll itself. How much grip will it provide? And if you brake on the roll, will your tyres actually grip?

The granite rolls at many of the 7stanes trail centres in Scotland offer fantastic grip, even when wet. Other surfaces such as the wooden stunts at the Glentress Freeride track are less forgiving in the wet and can send your bike sideways under braking. Cedar is the only wood that is naturally grippy.

Try it. It is vital to approach the roll in the attack position. Keep nice and relaxed and look ahead. Having scoped out the roll beforehand you should know your entry point. If it is a wide entry, use a visual marker like a stone or tuft of grass to make sure you roll down your chosen line - it will be hard to change your line when you're over the edge. Once safely onto the roll, shift your weight according to the gradient

of the slope. The steeper the roll the further back your weight should be, although not so far back that you lose control of the front end. You will use your brakes on a steep roll, but be gentle: too much and your weight will be pitched forward. The steeper the roll, the less braking required. Look ahead for your exit and be ready for the transition back to the trail.

When entering a steep roll, point your toes up slightly. This helps to keep you steady and prevent your feet slipping off - particularly if you hit uneven terrain.

The mechanics of jumping

Correct weight shift and a little confidence will ensure that jumping is not just for the experts

More confident riders are often eager to graduate to jumping - a skill that may look difficult but, when broken down, is well within the reach of many beginners. This is because jumping is best achieved using weight transfer, a concept already covered at length in chapter three. With this understanding and a little practice, you will be airborne in no time.

To start, it is best to practise on a small tabletop jump with a good surface. A nice

even jump with an equal gradient on both the up slope and the down slope is perfect. The top of the table should also be long enough to fit both wheels.

To ensure correct weight shift, keep the speed right down so you have time to think through what you are doing. Don't worry about getting your wheels off the ground at this point: it is more important that you can shift your weight, reacting to the jump as you roll over it.

If the front wheel feels too light and unstable, your weight is not far enough forward. Likewise, if the bike is bucking you as it reaches the lip of the jump, too much of your weight is at the rear. In both cases, shift your weight forward by moving your hips towards the bars.

Try it. Roll towards the up slope in the attack position with sufficient momentum to get you over the jump without pedalling. Shift your weight forward on the up slope so that it remains over the centre of the bike. As the front wheel runs over the lip of the jump, the bike will start to level out. At this point, shift your weight again to keep it central and return to the attack position when both wheels are on top of the jump. Then, as the bike rolls down the back slope, shift your weight backwards but remain central over the bottom bracket. Stay tall and relaxed and really concentrate on your forwards and backwards movement - not up and down. Once you get the hang of this at slow speed, put a bit more momentum into it and try two tabletop jumps in succession using the same technique.

Push and spring jumps

**Once you have mastered the weight shift needed for jumps, it is
time to get really airborne**

Now that you are comfortable shifting
your weight over a jump, it is time to
introduce up and down movement to help
you get the wheels off the ground. Getting
'air' is all about using your body as a spring
to generate extra lift as you go over the lip

of a jump. It takes some practice, but the
results can be spectacular.

There are two key steps to getting
airborne: the crouch and the release.
As you approach the up slope, shift your
weight towards the front of the bike and

*Build up gradually. If you find your front
wheel becoming light and uncontrolled
or your weight being pitched forward
then go back a step and just roll the
jump to regain your rhythm.*

crouch down by bending your arms and legs. As you roll to the lip of the jump, start to extend first your arms and then your legs aiming to straighten up as you go over the lip. Straightening the arms first followed by the legs helps to achieve a nice smooth arc in the air. Think of it like a gazelle jumping - although you might not be quite so graceful to begin with.

Try it. Remember to keep your head up and look where you are going to avoid wobble. Practise degrees of crouch and release as your confidence grows. To get more air, just push the bike into the slope harder - energy that gets paid back in spades when you extend and leave the lip.

Tackling awkward terrain

Break tricky sections of trail down into bite-size chunks and your task will seem much easier

Even the best riders can be unnerved by particularly awkward sections of trail. However, by breaking a challenging section down into bite-size chunks and applying your essential skills, it will become much easier to negotiate.

Try to constantly ask yourself questions about the trail and think through the weight transfer required for each section. Does the trail continually change gradient? Perhaps it gets particularly steep in places, or even turns into a full-on climb. Think ahead and adjust your weight accordingly.

In addition, a trail that is challenging underfoot requires a degree of momentum to keep you safe. If you roll over a section of trail too slowly, it will feel like your wheel is catching every root and stone.

A bit of extra momentum will keep you upright.

Be sure to also keep your eyes looking up, constantly scanning the trail well beyond your front wheel: doing so has the sensation of slowing down time, giving you more opportunity to plan your next moves.

But most important of all, stay relaxed. If rigid, all the muscles in your arms and shoulders tense resulting in very little movement of the bike. Expect the unexpected and don't worry about it. The bike will move around beneath you, especially if the surface is loose, but if you keep your eyes ahead and stay relaxed then you will be in much better control of where you want to go.

An obvious first reaction when a rider is challenged is to reach for the brakes. Go easy: if brakes are pulled sharply when in motion they can provide an unwelcome lesson in physics. Try to use the skills you have learned and trust them to get you through tricky sections.

Creating the flow

Now it is time to put the pieces together to create real flow - that perfect combination of technique, speed and grace

Creating real flow on a ride is a mountain biker's Holy Grail. It is that time when a section of trail just feels right: you nail every corner, float over every jump and pop every root. There are times when you get to the end of a section and are blown away by how well you rode.

Such flow can be achieved by successfully combining the skills you have worked on in this book, with good body movement at the core of everything you do. Such movement should be fluid and graceful. You are much heavier than the bike, so if you twitch or lurch, your bike will do the same.

Use a familiar, simple section of trail to work on creating the flow - something like Blue Velvet at Glentress is perfect (see sidebar). It is a blue-graded trail with nice sweeping corners and features that allow riders to put skills to use without being overloaded with rocks, roots, or an unpredictable surface.

Run through and warm up physically and mentally. While riding, move backwards and forwards to begin with, before introducing up and down movement, using your body to push the bike into the trail.

By moving around the bike you can apply pressure at different points, such as where you need more grip (remember squashing your 'O'). Try to really experiment with

bringing your weight forward and down - a real progression from the weight transfer outlined in chapter three. Once these body movements begin to feel smooth, you can apply the same techniques to more difficult terrain.

And don't forget to apply your other skills: braking and gearing efficiently, looking ahead, cornering with your body and more. By putting all the skills together, you will be in total control and just might put in the ride of your life.

Blue Velvet is one of our favourite trails at Glentress. Not long after it was finished, World Cup Downhill champion Tracy Moseley came to stay. We went for a pedal and did a loop that incorporated Blue Velvet. We got to the end of the trail just in time to see Tracy flying around the last corner with a huge grin on her face. She may have been a World Cup winner riding one of the 'easiest' trails in the forest, but she was blown away. According to Tracy, Blue Velvet was the ideal trail to practise core cornering and foundation skills. And so we end with probably the best tip of all: keep it simple.

glossary

Berm a steeply banked corner, built up to allow riders to corner at speed

Bombhole just as it sounds - steep drop into a hole, followed by a steep but short run back out

Chicken run a little section of trail, usually off to the side of a jump or drop-off, that provides an alternative to the scary stuff

Clips/SPD SPD stands for Shimano Pedalling Dynamics and has become the generic term for pedals that attach to cycling-specific shoes (hence 'clipped in')

Doubles two jumps, like camel bumps, one immediately after the other

Drop-off a sheer drop, which can either be jumped or - providing it's not too severe - rolled over, dropping the front wheel first

Flats pedals that are just a platform to rest your feet on rather than be clipped in

Full suss bike with front and rear suspension

Fun park sections of downhill singletrack where features such as jumps, tabletops, doubles, berms, etc. come thick and fast

Hardtail bike with no rear suspension

MTB abbreviation for a mountain bike

North Shore raised timber trails which appear at a number of centres in Scotland. They owe their name to their Canadian origins, where they are used to cross wet or boggy ground

Rock garden rocks embedded in the ground to provide a bone-jarring ride

Rock steps varying sizes, usually a single step uphill

Roots tree roots: a common obstacle on the trails in Scotland and potentially hazardous as they can be very slippy

Singletrack the ultimate mountain bike riding experience: trails not much wider than your tyres

Switchbacks uphill or downhill corners that come back on themselves

Tabletop like a double but with the middle bit filled in to leave a flat top suitable either for rolling over or jumping, to land on the down side